Four-Play

A play

Colin Smith

Samuel French—London
New York-Toronto-Hollywood

FOUR-PLAY

First performed under the title *Quartet* by St. Patrick's Dramatic
Society, Dalkey with the following cast:

David	Don Briggs
Caroline	Hilda Grace
Helen	Carmel McCrea
Edward	Peter Beamish

Directed by Michael Stokes

Subsequently performed at the Bray One-Act Theatre Festival
(where it won the overall award) with the following cast:

David	Don Briggs
Caroline	Phil Stokes
Helen	Fran Durie
Edward	Peter Beamish

Directed by Colin Smith

CHARACTERS

David
Caroline, married to David
Helen
Edward, married to Helen

The action of the play takes place in the sitting-room of David's and Caroline's house

Time — the present

FOUR-PLAY

Scene 1

The sitting-room of David's and Caroline's house. Evening

There are two doors to the room; one leads to the kitchen, one to the hallway. The room has a sofa, armchairs, a sideboard, a coffee table with newspapers on it, a stereo unit with tapes

Before the Curtain *rises, music plays; a very loud orchestral piece*

The Curtain *rises. David is setting out bottles (whisky, sherry, brandy and liqueurs), glasses, etc. on the sideboard*

Caroline enters from the kitchen with a portable phone

Caroline (*shouting over the music*) David! (*She pauses; then, louder*) David!

David (*turning down the music*) What?

Caroline Turn that down, will you? I can't hear Sarah on the phone.

David Sorry. (*He turns off the music*)

Caroline That's better. (*Into the phone*) All right, Sarah, now don't worry, darling, I'll look after Teddy for you. Listen, I'm giving him a good-night kiss. (*She makes a kissing noise into the phone*) Happy, now? (*She pauses*) Everything all right?

David Tell her I sent my love.

Caroline (*into the phone*) OK, now, don't worry. ... Sarah, we'll be collecting you from the bus tomorrow afternoon. Have a lovely time. Daddy sends his love. (*She pauses*) Bye. (*She shuts off the phone; angrily*) Bloody hell, as if I didn't have enough things to worry about.

David What was all that about?

Caroline Sarah forgot to take her Teddy to camp. You should have heard the fuss she made.

Caroline exits to the kitchen

David Well, she's only eight, and it is her first time away from home.

Caroline (*off; grudgingly*) Yes, I suppose so.

David Kevin go off all right?

Caroline (*off*) Yes. No thanks to you.

David (*approaching the door*) All right, I've said ——

Caroline enters with dishes of crisps, peanuts, etc.. During the following she goes in and out of the kitchen, clearing the papers off the coffee table and laying out the dishes of nibbles

You promised to be home in time to take him round to Pauline's.

David I said I was ——

Caroline These are your friends coming tonight as well as mine, you know. I think you could make some effort and not leave me to do everything.

David All right. I've said I'm sorry. I was delayed.

Caroline Don't forget to open the wine.

David I did it ages ago, when I came in.

Caroline What?

David That's what's recommended. Have it open in the room where it's going to be served one or two hours before using.

Caroline Never thought you'd become a wine snob. When we were in France, you drank nothing but rotgut out of plastic bottles. (*She inserts a new tape in the tape player of the stereo and switches on*)

David OK, OK. I've just got more interested in wine. That's it.

A Phil Coulter track plays

Caroline Sure it's not just to impress our well-off friends?

David (*though it is the truth*) Not at all.

Caroline (*amused*) Liar.

Caroline moves to exit

(*As she goes*) I'd better get back to the kitchen. I'm way behind.

Caroline exits

David switches off the tape with an exasperated sigh

Caroline (*off*) Hey, I like that.
David Well I don't.
Caroline (*off*) David!
David If we're going to have music, let's have something a bit better than that.
Caroline (*off*) There's nothing wrong with ——
David That's not real music, that's what they play in lifts and supermarkets. Wallpaper for the ears.

Caroline appears in the kitchen doorway

Caroline Well, excuse me for my low tastes.
David Come on, Caroline, you know what I mean. There's no depth to it, no feeling. It ——
Caroline (*moving to the tape deck*) Damn you, David, don't start preaching to me about music again. I know you like serious stuff. I know you love opera. I know you have a bloody season ticket for the Concert Hall.
David Look, don't fly off the handle.
Caroline (*overriding him*) You don't have to lecture me about it all the time. Just for once in my life let me put on a tape I like which won't require everybody's full and reverent attention in total silence and might just might help make the atmosphere a little welcoming. (*She angrily switches on the tape*)

The Phil Coulter music begins again, very loudly

David OK, OK, I'm sorry ...

The doorbell rings

Caroline Oh shit, they're here. You let them in, I've still got a
couple of things to do.

Caroline exits into the kitchen

David Bloody hell. This is a fine way to start an evening. (*He turns
down the music's volume*)

David exits to the front door

We hear the distant sound of the front door opening

(*Off*) Hi, Helen. Come on in. Good to see you. Where's Edward?

Helen enters, followed by David

Helen He dropped me off. He had to go round by the hospital to
check on a patient. He won't be long.
David What'll you have to drink? Sherry?
Helen Yes, please.

David pours Helen a glass of sherry

This room looks lovely. Caroline has such marvellous taste.

David gives the glass of sherry to Helen

David Here you are. (*He pauses; then, quietly*) Hallo.
Helen (*equally softly*) Hallo, darling.

They kiss gently

David You all right?
Helen I suppose so. I wish this evening were over. (*She laughs
nervously*)

There is a slightly awkward pause

David I'm sorry ... This afternoon ... I shouldn't have ...
Helen Shh. (*She lays a finger across his mouth*) I was there too, remember.
David Yes, but ——
Helen I can't pretend I haven't thought about it happening long before this. You're a very good-looking man, you know. But then I didn't think you'd be interested in somebody nearly five years older than you, and not very — well — glamorous. (*She again laughs nervously*)
David (*smiling*) It must be love, then.
Helen It must be. (*She smiles back, reassured*)
David I suppose our timing could have been better.
Helen Yes. The afternoon of the day your wife has asked us to dinner is hardly the best ——
David Shh. She's coming.

Helen quickly moves to a chair and sits

(*Pouring himself a glass of whisky*) How long did Edward think he'd be?
Helen Just a couple of minutes.

Caroline enters from kitchen

Caroline!
Caroline Helen, how are you? We haven't seen you in ages.
Helen Fine, thanks.

Caroline and Helen embrace

You're looking marvellous as usual. And so slim, how do you do it?
Caroline Well, I'm playing squash twice a week now. That keeps me fairly fit.
Helen How are the children?

Caroline Full of beans. Sarah's off at a Brownie camp and I farmed
Kevin out to a friend for the night.

Helen He's a gorgeous kid. When does he start school?

Caroline Next September. I'll have a G and T please, David.

David Right.

Caroline Edward on his way?

Helen Yes. I was just telling David he had to call over to the
hospital. There's an emergency patient he has to check on.

David sits

Caroline That's a shame. Does that happen very often?

Helen It seems to have got worse the last few months. Sometimes
he's called out several evenings in the week. But, hopefully, now
that he's got this new post, it'll mean some of the pressure will be
taken off.

Caroline Well, that's why we've asked you round. To celebrate.
(*She salutes Helen with her glass*) Congratulations to you both.

David Maybe you should wait till Edward gets here, before offering
congratulations.

Caroline (*sarcastically*) Sorry, darling. Oops, Caroline has made
another mistake. Excuse me, Helen, I'll take this drink in with me.
I've got a hot stove to slave over for a few minutes.

Helen Can I give you a hand?

Caroline Not at all. I'll only be a moment.

Caroline exits

Helen Is there a row?

David Yes.

Helen She doesn't suspect ...

David No, no. We just had a bit of a row about this bloody tape. (*He
gets up and switches the tape off*) She thinks this is high-class
quality classical music and doesn't see it for the pedestrian
rubbish it is.

Helen Oh?

David No, that's not fair. She knows it's just pleasant tuneful stuff
and she likes it, it's just ... It's one of the things we don't have in
common. One of the things we don't share.

Helen (*sighing*) I know what you mean.

David There seem to be a lot of those lately. (*He pauses*) Since you
and I became — close — I seem to find a lot of things about her
that annoy the hell out of me which before never bothered me.

Helen (*after a pause*) What are we going to do?

David I don't know. This — with you ... I never expected it to
develop as it has. We've known each other for five, six years and
why should we suddenly find ourselves "having an affair"?

Helen Are you regretting ... ?

David No, of course not. Don't think that. It's just that I thought I
had a happy marriage. You seemed to have one ...

Helen I do ... Did.

David And the last thing I want is to hurt her or ——

The doorbell rings

Edward.

*We hear the front door open and Edward's and Caroline's voices,
off*

David (*rising to the door; low and quickly*) Here they come. I'll
phone you tomorrow.

Helen (*low, quickly*) All right.

Edward enters carrying a bottle of wine. Caroline follows

Edward (*as he enters*) ... beautiful as ever, Caroline. David, how are
you? Sorry I'm so late, but people get sick at the most inconven-
ient times. Here's a little something for your burgeoning wine
cellar. I hear you're getting interested in claret as a hobby.

David (*taking bottle*) Edward, you shouldn't have. This is far
too ——

Edward Don't worry. I didn't buy it here. It was part of a selection that our wine club put together a few years ago when the growth was young.

David Even so.

Edward Enjoy. Enjoy.

David Thanks, then. What'll you have to drink?

Edward Scotch, if you have it. No ice, no water. Just itself.

David pours a whisky for Edward

Helen Excuse me for a moment, Caroline, I'll just nip up to the bathroom.

Caroline Of course. David, dinner any time. You and Edward bring your drinks in when you're ready.

Helen and Caroline exit

Edward (*sinking into a chair, tired*) Aah! Let me sit down for a sec, I've been on my feet all day. (*He drinks*) Just what the doctor ordered.

David Congratulations on getting the new post, Edward. You must be delighted.

Edward Thanks, David. Yes, I'm very pleased. The research work will be interesting, and there should be a lot less pressure.

David When do you take it up?

Edward First of the month. (*He pauses*) David ... While the girls are out, can I talk to you about something?

David Sure.

Edward David ... I'm not sure how to put this. I mean it seems ridiculous somehow, but ... I mean, Helen's the best in the world, but, dammit, she's not Jane Fonda. I can't see ...

David What are you getting at?

Edward I think Helen's having an affair with someone.

David (*after a short pause*) Edward, I don't ——

Edward You see. You don't think it's likely either. But over the past year — things haven't been quite the same at home. I mean we still — you know, enjoy bed and so on — but she seems to have distanced herself from me somehow. Erected some sort of a wall.

David I'm sure you're mistaken, Edward.

Edward I don't think so. I've started to notice things which don't seem to add up. Appointments she hasn't kept. A friend rang up once for a chat when I thought Helen was with her. Even this afternoon ——

David I'm sure ...

Edward Oh, there was always a reasonable explanation but when I look back I feel I can see some sort of a pattern forming. And I don't like it.

David Have you talked to her? Have you said anything about this?

Edward No, I couldn't. I hadn't the nerve. Funny, I'm usually the one full of confidence. No problem facing up to things, but I think — if it were true — if I thought Helen had stopped loving ... Sorry, David, to unload this on you, but I had to get it off my chest. We've known you for a long time, and I needed someone to talk to. Someone who'd make me see what an idiot I am. (*He laughs*)

David I'm sorry, Edward, I ——

Helen enters

Helen Well, you two, Caroline sends her compliments, and would the gentlemen care to join us?

David Right, Helen. Just coming. Edward?

Edward (*draining his glass*) On my way.

Helen heads for the exit

Helen (*as she goes*) They're coming, Caroline.

Helen exits

Edward (*quietly*) Not a word to Caroline, David. Please.

David Of course not. Edward, I'm sure there's nothing in it ...

Edward Thanks, David. I feel a bit better, just to have talked to you about it. (*He sighs; then, brightly*) Here we go, then. The condemned man ate a hearty seven-course dinner.

Edward and David exit, laughing

Black-out

Music plays, swiftly increasing in volume

SCENE 2

The music fades

The Lights come up

*All four are sitting, relaxed, after dinner, having coffee and liqueurs.
David holds a bottle of brandy. They are all laughing*

David Some more brandy, Edward?
Edward Don't mind if I do.

David takes Edward's glass and refills it

   That was a marvellous meal, Caroline.
David (*holding out Edward's glass*) Here you are.
Caroline (*to Edward*) Thank you, kind sir.
Edward (*taking the glass*) Thanks, David.
David Another drink for you, Helen?
Helen No, thanks.
David Caroline?
Caroline Yes, please.

David pours Caroline another drink during the following

Edward I suppose you heard about Sally and Michael?
Caroline What about them?
Edward They've agreed to split up.
David That's a shame.
Caroline Why do you say that? They've been heading for a break-
   up for years.
David I didn't think things were that serious.
Edward Apparently so. Sally found out Michael had been seeing
   this other woman for months. So she confronted him with it. To
   make a long story short, he swore he'd give her up. Said it was all
   over, nothing serious, so on and so forth. Sally dug in her heels,
   and said she wasn't going to take second place. If he wanted to
   play around, he could do it somewhere else. So goodbye, Michael.

Caroline Well, good for Sally.

Helen You don't mean that, surely, Caroline.

Caroline Of course I mean it. Why should she put up with treatment like that? How would you feel? I know if I found David was playing around I'd do exactly the same.

Edward That's a bit harsh, Caroline.

Caroline I don't think so. Nobody should have to endure the insult of being cheated on like that.

Edward But do you not think there's such a thing as forgive and forget?

Caroline Not in this sort of case. Look, Edward, I'm not getting all uptight about the holy sacrament of marriage or anything, but if two people have an arrangement, an agreement — all right, a promise, to live together and support each other ——

David (*sarcastically*) A mutual life support system. That's what marriage is all about.

Caroline It's not something to joke about, David. But, in fact you're right, it is a mutual support system. It's a fairly delicate system too, and needs an equal amount of commitment from both sides. If one partner decides not to give it that commitment, then the other is quite justified in saying "Piss off".

Edward (*teasingly*) Hey, Caroline.

Caroline Sorry, Edward, it just gets to me, that's all. Everywhere you look you see marriages breaking up. Nobody seems to take the thing seriously any more. Sometimes I think the whole population of the Western world is primarily occupied in leaping in and out of each other's beds ...

David (*to lighten the atmosphere*) It's a wonder they get any work done.

Caroline For Christ's sake, David, I'm being serious.

David Take it easy, Caroline, it was only a joke. Another drop, Edward?

Edward No thanks, David. Got to drive soon.

Caroline It's not something to joke about, David.

David (*dismissively*) Simmer down, Caroline. You'll have another, Helen.

Helen No thanks.

David Oh, go on. The night is young.

Caroline (*louder*) She said no, David. I'm sure she's old enough
to decide for herself.

David I was only making sure ——

Caroline — that she was being well looked after, I know. You're
really good at that, David, you really are. Make sure she's got the
best chair. Make sure she's not in a draught. Make sure she's got
enough to drink. Make sure she's happy in bed.

Silence. Edward sits totally still and silent throughout the following

David (*trying to smooth things over*) Caroline. Don't be ridiculous.
Helen, I'm sorry ...

Caroline Oh, David, stop it. I can't keep up this charade any longer.
I know, damn it. I know. Don't you understand? Your little secret
is out, darling. You don't have to hide it any more. Not that you
were very good at that anyway.

David You're talking rubbish, Caroline, I haven't ...

Caroline (*more quietly*) You're not a very good liar, David. And
you're not very good at hiding your feelings. It's been obvious for
months that something's going on. Little remarks. The way her
name keeps cropping up in conversation. I've seen the way you
look at her, David. I've damn well smelt her perfume after you've
been to one of your bloody symphony concerts.

Helen Caroline ... I'm ... It's not what you think.

Caroline Shut up, Helen. It is what I think.

Helen (*after a pause*) Edward ... Edward. (*She starts to cry, not
moving, not hiding it*) Oh God, I'm sorry, Edward. I didn't mean
to hurt you ... I couldn't help ... (*She tails off; whispering*) I love
him.

Silence

*Edward rises and moves to the sideboard. He picks up the whisky
bottle and gestures to David to ask if it is all right to take a drink*

Edward OK?

David (*confused*) Of course.

Edward (*pouring a drink*) Anyway, I suppose since you've had my wife, it's all right if I have your scotch.

David For Christ's sake ... (*He pauses; then, quietly*) I'm sorry, Edward.

Edward (*angrily*) Oh come on, David, don't talk crap. If you were that sorry you wouldn't have started it. You must have known what you were doing, both of you. You're not children. You're only sorry you've been found out.

There is a pause

David So what are we going to do?

Edward We?

David Well, now that my wife has decided to drag this out into the open and rub our noses in it, we can't just leave it. We must decide something.

Edward David, I don't think either you or Helen have any rights in this. Caroline and I are the ones to make any decisions that are going to be made. You've apparently made yours already.

Helen But Edward ...

Edward (*overriding her*) Caroline has already made her position perfectly clear. It's out on the street for you, David. Don't you remember? No commitment, no home comforts. And I must say, I'm inclined to agree with her.

Caroline Edward, I ... I'm not sure ... Look, Edward, I feel awful. I didn't mean to have this come out in the open the way it has. What I said before ... I was hoping that David would listen to my way of looking at things, and, well, get the message that I wasn't going to be walked on like a doormat. That if he kept on seeing —Helen, he'd better be prepared to take the consequences.

David She's going to change her mind. I might have known. (*He moves to the sideboard and prepares himself a fresh drink during the following*)

Edward You're saying you didn't mean what you said earlier?

Caroline I meant it that I think that Sally was perfectly within her rights to kick Michael out. That was right for her. But I — we — have children, and ——

David (*loudly*) Caroline. I think you're just bloody scared. All this crap about throwing me out. You're scared that I'm going to walk out, that you'll be left to fend for yourself. You're thinking of yourself, aren't you, what you're going to live on. Who's going to pay the mortgage? Little things like that.

Edward Hang on, David.

Caroline God, David, you can be vicious when you want to be. I don't know why I want to hang on to this marriage.

David Well, why do you? You were full of claptrap about partnerships and promises being broken, and no second chances.

Caroline Because it was a promise, damn it. Better or worse. Sickness and health, remember?

David Oh, don't be so bloody ridiculous. People change. We're not the same people we were when we got married. Our views have changed, our ideas. Our circumstances are different. We've grown up, for heaven's sake.

Edward But it's supposed to be for life, David. You're supposed to realize that at the time. You're supposed to make some sort of effort to keep the thing going.

David But you can't regard marriage as a life sentence, not in this day and age. You must have the right to make a change, if you meet someone else, fall in love with someone else, who means much more to you than your present partner ——

Edward Like my wife.

David (*stopped in mid-flow, more quietly*) Yes. Like your wife. Look, Edward, I'm sorry, sorry as hell, but it just happened. I — we didn't plan it.

Edward (*sarcastically*) It just happened.

David Yes.

Edward Just by accident. A chance meeting in town. "Fancy meeting you, let's have a cup of coffee", and you have a very enjoyable time, you never realized before what good company she was. Then a couple of phone calls "just for a chat". Meet for lunch? Why not? Better not mention it at home though, just in case she gets the wrong idea. Going to the opera? Well, why not get two tickets. Wife hates that sort of thing and what harm if we ——

David How did you know? You couldn't have known.

Edward (*wearily*) David, David, did you think you were the first man to be attracted to someone outside marriage? This goes on all the time. Look around you. (*He pauses*) And I'm not a saint, I'm afraid, I've been there too.

Helen ⎱ (*together*) ⎰ What?
Caroline ⎰   ⎱ Edward!

Edward Yes, Helen, I never thought I'd have to admit it, but I'm afraid it's true. It was a very long time ago, and she's married now and living abroad, but I know how you feel, David. It's rotten, isn't it? Life's a bitch. How did I get into this mess of a marriage? Why can't I just ride away into the sunset with my beloved while the full orchestra swells up into a triumphant finale?

David Don't be so bloody facetious, Edward.

Caroline But you didn't.

Edward No, Caroline, I didn't. I thought about it, I must confess. I considered all the options. It wouldn't have been so hard at the time. We've no children. Money no problem. Helen has plenty of her own, as you know, and she wouldn't have had to worry on that score. I could have taken off, free as air.

David So why not?

Helen Why not, Edward?

Edward It was a pretty close thing. At least it seemed so at the time, but looking back I know it couldn't have turned out any other way. She went away for a while — a cooling-off period, you might say.

Caroline And did it work?

Edward Well, it did cool off, on my side at least. But it wasn't a question of "out of sight, out of mind" just like that. I worked at it. I made a deliberate effort to rebuild our marriage.

Caroline How?

Edward Well, I tried to pay more attention to Helen, to think more positively about the good things we had together. I suppose you could say I had too much respect for Helen to just let what was between us die. Too much invested in the partnership. And I know it sounds dreadfully corny, but — (*he shrugs apologetically*) too much love.

David And now?

Edward Still too much love. So, whatever has happened between you two makes no difference. (*He pauses*) Well, not too much.

Caroline You'll forgive her?

Edward I don't think it's a matter of forgiving so much. Just absorbing it.

Helen (*rising and standing over Edward*) By heaven, Edward, you really can be a sanctimonious bastard when you want to be. All this talk of forgiving and absorbing. It just makes you feel good about yourself, that's all. You've had a nice little fling and now so have I, so now it's all square, is it? Let's throw the dice and have another go.

Edward Helen, that's enough.

Helen It may be enough for you, but not for me. I haven't had enough. I've found something I want, and I'm not going to let it go. I don't care who's in the way or who's going to be hurt. I'm not giving up. I'm going to have him.

David gets up and restrains Helen

David Take it easy, Helen.

Helen shakes David off

Helen (*to Edward*) Who do you think you are, preaching to me? You sit there and calmly tell me you had an affair with someone but it was years ago, and you've managed to get over it so come on, Helen, old girl, get a grip on yourself, and stop this little bit of foolishness.

Edward (*sharply*) Helen. Stop it.

Helen (*fiercely*) I won't stop it. It's all right for you. It's fine for you. You go off to work every day. You meet people. You talk. You're kept occupied. You're useful. You come home in the evening and you're too tired, too concerned with outside things to talk to me, to share, to be interested in me, in my thoughts, my ideas, my boring, stupid, unimportant, silly boring day.

Edward Helen. We've been through this before.

Helen And we're going through it again. David talks to me. He doesn't shrug me off. He listens, he pays attention. He doesn't dismiss my ideas as unimportant.

Caroline (*sotto voce*) He sounds marvellous.

David Stop it, Caroline.

Helen (*becoming hysterical as the speech progresses*) He's too good for you anyway. David's got a mind. He needs more than endless chatter about cosmetics and clothes and squash games and babies and school reports and how well Sarah is doing in her dancing classes.

Edward grabs Helen by the shoulders

Edward Helen. Stop it. Now.

Edward slaps Helen's cheek. She subsides into her chair, crying

David Christ, Edward, did you have to do that?

Edward Stay out of this David. (*He crouches down by Helen's chair*) Helen, it'll be all right ... Helen.

Helen (*still sobbing*) You hit me.

Edward Ssshh, Helen. (*He moves to put his arm around Helen*) Everything will be all right ... Helen.

Helen Take your hands off me.

Edward Helen ...

Helen Damn you, let me go.

Helen rises and runs out of the room

Silence

Caroline (*quietly*) That's what all this is about, is it?

David (*in state of shock*) What?

Edward I think so.

David What? What the hell are you talking about?

Caroline Children, mainly, I should think ...

David What do you mean?

Caroline She wants a child, David, a family. (*She pauses*) A reason for living.

Edward And she can't. Well, I can't.

Caroline And she thought that David would do nicely as a substitute.

Edward Maybe.

David But that's crazy. Are you trying to tell me she started an affair with me because she wanted a child?

Edward Not consciously, of course. But I'd say sub-consciously that may have been one of the contributing factors to the — attraction — you had for her.

David That's ridiculous.

Edward Maybe. Helen is not a well woman, David. We've obviously never talked about it, but for a number of years now she's been having some treatment for ... Well, actually it's none of your business.

Caroline I'm sorry, Edward, I didn't know.

Edward Anyway, children are out of the question. As I've said, I have problems in that department. And it would be too late for her now anyway. It wouldn't be safe at her age.

David But she's only ...

Edward She's nearly fifty, David.

David But she told me ...

Edward She's fifty next May, David, whatever she told you.

David (*after a short pause; then, quietly*) I don't believe it. (*He moves to the sideboard and pours himself a drink*)

Edward Caroline, I'd better see if she's all right.

Caroline Of course.

Edward exits

Pause

Caroline Will you get me a gin while you're there?

David grunts assent

David, we need to talk.

David Oh God, Caroline, don't start lecturing me, I couldn't stand it.

Caroline Stop feeling so sorry for yourself, for heaven's sake, and try and face up to the mess you've got yourself in. And me too. Like it or not, we're in this together. And you've got to make up your mind on a few things.

David Go on.

David hands Caroline a drink

Caroline She said she loves you. Do you love her?

David Yes.

Caroline Why?

David What do you mean why? What kind of a question is that?

Caroline A pretty basic one, I should think.

David I can't say why. Not just like that — to you anyway.

Caroline Listen, David. We've been married for nearly ten years and we practically lived together for months before that. Things were good between us. We have two children. Their lives are important too. You can't just walk away from them.

David I'm not walking away.

Caroline Well they're certainly not in the forefront of your mind.

David Look, Caroline, let's not start talking as if we're going to get divorced over this. I've no intention ... (*he stops short, realizing what he has said*) I mean ....

Caroline Go on, David.

David You have to understand that this has happened almost without me realizing it. It really was a bit like Edward said. We met a couple of times at concerts. We went for a drink and a chat, and — just — we got on well together. Seemed to think alike about so many things. You and I were going through a bad patch at the time and I found her company refreshing.

Caroline David, I don't really want to hear a rose-coloured, blow by blow account of your romance. Look at it from my point of view. You've been making a fool of me, telling me lies, coming to bed with me after sleeping with her ——

David (*quickly*) No.

Caroline What do you mean, no?

David I didn't do that.

Caroline You mean you ——
David Only once. This afternoon was the first time ...

There is a pause

Caroline I don't believe it.
David It's true.
Caroline I don't believe it. (*She starts to laugh*)
David You must believe it. I hadn't intended to go that ...
Caroline (*laughing*) Poor David. Poor old David. One slip and the whole world comes crashing down around your head.
David For God's sake, Caroline, it's not bloody funny.
Caroline (*recovering*)No. No, of course it's not. I'm sorry.
David Look, I've been trying to explain ——
Caroline Did you enjoy it?
David What?
Caroline You heard me. Was it enjoyable?
David I can't ... I'm not going to ...
Caroline (*softly*) It wasn't really, was it?

There is a pause. It is obvious that David will not respond

You really have got yourself in a mess, haven't you?
David (*after a long sigh*) Yes.
Caroline (*quietly*) Think hard about this, David. Have you thought at all seriously about — living with her, rather than me. Anything like that. Or have you just been going on from day to day, letting things happen, enjoying the experience, without thinking or planning.

There is a pause

Have you?
David I suppose I have. Just drifted on, I mean, it was all so ... I felt happy.
Caroline Yes, well, let's not get too carried away. The point is, can you stop? (*She pauses*) Do you want to? (*She pauses; then, softly*) I'll help, if you want to try.

Silence. David takes Caroline's hand

David Thanks.

Silence. We hear Edward, off, coming to the door

    Edward enters

    I'm taking Helen home, Caroline. She's been sick, I'm afraid. I've cleaned up and everything, but I'd better get her home.
David Edward.
Edward Yes?
David I'd like to take her out to the car.

Edward hesitates

    Please?

Edward steps away from the door

    David exits

Edward I suppose we should let them say goodbye in private.
Caroline So long as it's goodbye for good.
Edward No doubt about it. I know Helen. She's too much pride to let herself continue after what's been said here tonight.
Caroline It was quite a wearing experience.
Edward I wouldn't want to go through it again. I know we agreed that attack would be the best form of defence, but it was getting a bit close there for a while.
Caroline Well, I couldn't take the risk of David dumping me. I'd be stranded without a penny. And with two brats to support, what kind of life would I have?
Edward And we know Helen's lawyers would skin me for every cent if it came to a divorce. I'm not complaining, Caroline, we agreed their fling had to be stopped, no matter how. I didn't think David would swallow the bit about her being mentally unstable, though.

Caroline By that time he'd have swallowed anything.

There is a pause. Edward swallows the last of his drink and puts his glass on the sideboard

Caroline Tomorrow?
Edward (*smiling*) Of course. It's Thursday, isn't it?
Caroline Of course.

They kiss, hungrily

Goodnight, love.

Edward exits

Caroline sits to finish her drink

Music plays

CURTAIN

FURNITURE AND PROPERTY LIST

SCENE 1

On stage: Sofa
Armchairs
Sideboard. *On it*: glasses; bottles of whisky, sherry, brandy
    and liqueurs
Coffee table. *On it*: newspapers
Stereo unit with tapes

Off stage: Portable phone (**Caroline**)
Dishes of crisps, peanuts, etc.(**Caroline**)
Bottle of wine (**Edward**)

SCENE 2

On stage: Four coffee cups and saucers
Coffee pot, cream jug, sugar bowl, etc.

LIGHTING PLOT

Practical fittings required: nil
One interior. The same throughout

Scene 1

To open: General interior lighting

Cue 1   **Edward** and **David** exit laughing; music   (Page 9)
             Black-out

Scene 2

To open: General interior lighting

No cues

EFFECTS PLOT

Cue 1   When ready   (Page 1)
           Very loud orchestral music

Cue 2   **David** turns down the music   (Page 1)
           Reduce volume of music

Cue 3   **David** switches off the orchestral music   (Page 2)
           Cut orchestral music

Cue 4   **Caroline** switches the tape player on   (Page 2)
           A few seconds of silent lead-in, then a Phil Coulter track

Cue 5   **David** switches off the tape   (Page 3)
           Cut music

Cue 6   **Caroline** switches on the tape   (Page 3)
           Phil Coulter track, very loud

Cue 7   **David**: "OK, OK, I'm sorry ..."   (Page 4)
           Doorbell

Cue 8   **David** turns down the music's volume   (Page 4)
           Reduce volume of music

Cue 9   **David** switches the tape off   (Page 6)
           Cut music

Cue 10   **David**: " ... is to hurt her or ——"   (Page 7)
           Doorbell rings

Cue 11   **Edward** and **David** exit laughing   (Page 9)
           Music plays, swiftly increasing in volume

Cue 12   As Scene 2 begins   (Page 10)
           Fade music

Cue 13   **Caroline** sits to finish her drink   (Page 22)
           Music plays